David's Magic Ears

By Barbara Hinyard
Illustrated by Yasushi Matsuoka

ISBN: 9781087887562

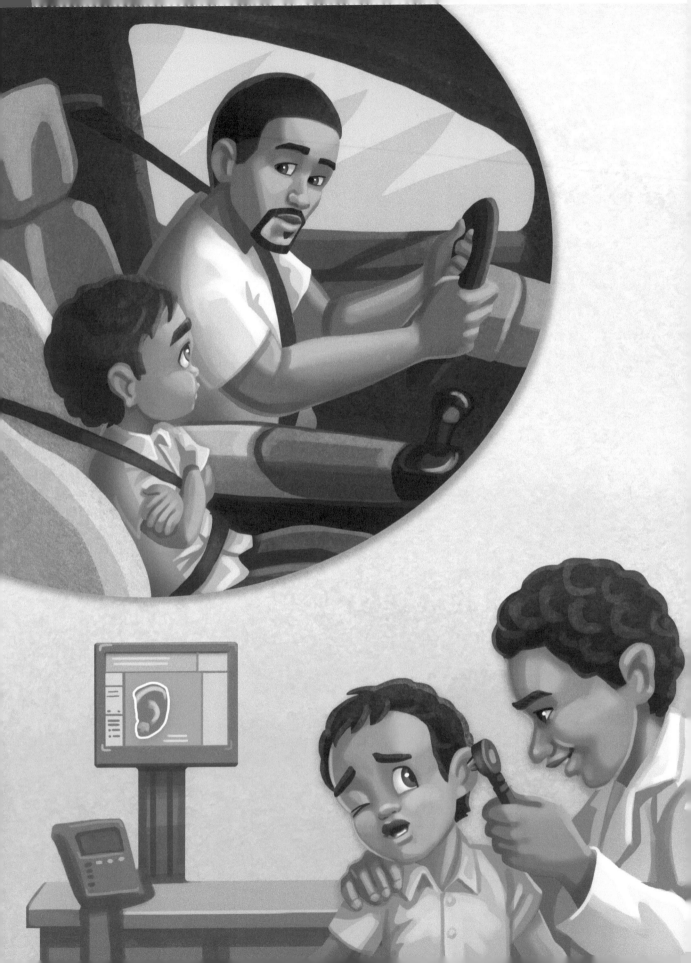

David sank down in the passenger seat of his father's car as he drove them off from the audiologist.

They just got news that he has a mild hearing loss and the audiologist says he needs hearing aids.

While he was there, the audiologist created molds in the shape of both of his ears.

David was curious about having to use hearing aids.

"Are you OK, Bunny?" his dad asked him.

"Yea, I'm dad, what are hearing aids like?"

"Hearing aids are a small device placed in your ear to make sounds audible to someone with hearing loss its to help you hear better."

"A device? Device sounds big, is it that big?" David replied to his dad.

"No son, it's like the size of an air pod," he replied laughing.

"Can I play music with it?" David inquired.

"Well, I don't know. That should be my next question to the doctor, I pray it doesn't though, I don't want you damaging your remaining ear," he replied.

"How are you holding up?" He continued.

"I'm looking forward to having my Magic Ear, Dad," David replied and smiled.

David got to know more about the hearing aid and how he would have to start using his Magic Ears to process sounds.

He knew his life was going to change a little, but he was prepared for it and he was going to make the most out of his hearing loss.

His sister , Amani , came in his room that evening to check on her brother.

"What did the audiologist say ?"Amani asked.

"Well I have to go back tomorrow to get hearing aids," David explained.

"What are hearing aids?" Amani asked.

"A hearing aid is a small device that is placed in your ear to makes sound audible to someone with a hearing loss."

As they talked, David was very appreciative of how his sister was understanding and spent time with him.

The next day, David hopped out of bed.

"Today is the day I get my Magic Ears!" he exclaimed.

He took his bath and ran downstairs to meet his dad.

"Good morning," the audiologist greeted and smiled as David , and his dad entered the office.

"Good morning," David and his dad replied.

"OK, this is the hearing aid, I'm going to test it on him to check if it fits perfectly," the audiologist said standing up from his seat. He helped David put on the hearing aid.

"Can you hear me perfectly?" the audiologist asked. David was quiet for a while. His smile was wide and he responded, "I think this is the best day of my life".

The audiologist, his dad ,and his sister Amani could clearly see the joy on David's face.

"I'm going to talk to a lot of people today," David said hugging his dad. His dad hugged him back as he laughed at what he shared. He was so happy for his son.

For David, getting the hearing aid felt like heaven. He couldn't stop talking to his dad.

"Ok, slow down, Bunny. How are you feeling? Are you okay?" David's dad asked.

"I haven't felt this great in a long time, Dad," David replied with a smile across his face.

"You know, you will be a little bit different from your peers in school, right?" he expressed his concern.

"That's alright. Everybody is different, Dad. Charles wears glasses, Mary wears braces, and Sam has asthma. We are all different in our own unique way." God made just the way he want us to be. David replied, still wearing that big bright smile on his face.

David's dad knew from that day that his son was going to be just fine.

He knew that he would be just fine with relying on a device to hear.

He realized he was actually looking forward to explore this new world of hearing with David and his Magic Ear.

Help the musical note reach David's Magic ear.

START

GOAL

Ways To Communicate With Children With Hearing Loss

Always face, or be on the hearing aided side of the person when you talk to them

Think about the environment - lighting, clothing, background noise etc

Use facial expression and gesture to add meaning

Repeat and rephrase your communication

Request confirmation from the hearing impaired individual

Don't over articulate, but don't mumble either

Think about your own volume and rate when you speak

Set the context to help the person understand

Write things down or draw a picture if you cannot communicate your message with speech or sign

Always respond

Reward with a smile

Basic Sign Language

EAT

DRINK

MORE

ALL DONE

PLEASE

THANK YOU

TOILET

HELP

WORD SEARCH

DOCTOR
DAVID
SOUND

MUSIC
AMANI
MAGIC

AMERICAN
SIGN
LANGUAGE

HEARING AID
EAR MOULD
AUDIOLOGIST

```
V  A  B  G  M  U  S  I  C  Z  C  C
A  Z  R  R  Q  H  D  M  V  A  I  M
M  O  L  S  E  E  Y  A  T  U  Z  O
A  Q  A  B  A  A  D  G  E  D  I  A
N  O  R  R  R  Y  I  M  I  Y  M
I  Y  G  L  M  I  B  C  M  O  I  E
S  P  U  K  O  N  T  C  P  L  R  R
B  I  A  G  U  G  Y  M  D  O  I  I
M  V  G  I  L  A  K  A  T  G  N  C
I  Y  E  N  D  I  W  C  Q  I  X  A
L  S  O  U  N  D  O  U  E  S  B  N
D  A  V  I  D  D  R  F  U  T  O  N
```

Vocabulary

American Sign Language (ASL): a form of sign language developed in the US and used also in English-speaking parts of Canada.

Hearing Aid: a small device that fits in or on the ear, worn by a partially deaf person to amplify sound.

Earmold: An earmold is a plastic or silicone piece that is made to fit to a child's ear. The earmold has a short tube that is attached to the part of the hearing aid that sits behind the child's ear. The earmold sends sound from the hearing aid into the ear.

Cochlear Implants: A cochlear implant is a surgically placed device that can help a person with severe to profound hearing loss

Audiologist: an audiologist is a licensed hearing health care professional who specializes in the diagnosis and treatment of hearing loss and balance disorders in adults and children.

Lip Reading: Lip reading (or speech reading) is a building block that helps a child with hearing loss understand Speech. The child watches the movements of a speaker's mouth and face to understand what the speaker is saying.

Individualized Educational Plan (IEP) is a plan or program developed to ensure that a child who has a disability identified under the law and is attending an elementary or secondary educational institution receives specialized instruction and related services.

ABOUT THE AUTHOR

I can do all things through Christ who strengthens me.

Philippians 4:13

Barbara Hinyard is from Baton Rouge, Louisiana.
She has been writing since age 11.
Her twin inspired her to write her first poem.
Barbara enjoys working with children.
Working with children is her passion.

Printed in the USA
CPSIA information can be obtained
at www.ICGtesting.com
LVHW060758261123
764939LV00037B/334